Incredible Eddie

by Becky Cheston
illustrated by Susan Gaber

Harcourt
SCHOOL PUBLISHERS

Printed in China

ISBN 10: 0-15-350560-5
ISBN 13: 978-0-15-350560-7

Ordering Options
ISBN 10: 0-15-350335-1 (Grade 5 Below-Level Collection)
ISBN 13: 978-0-15-350335-1 (Grade 5 Below-Level Collection)
ISBN 10: 0-15-357561-1 (package of 5)
ISBN 13: 978-0-15-357561-7 (package of 5)

11 12 13 14 15 0940 12 11 10

Somewhere, a cage rattled. Everywhere, black noses poked through wire holes. Ten minutes ago, when he had first come in, Eddie had been happy. He had listened, inhaled, and adored every pup. Now, the longer he stood here, the worse he felt.

"Isn't this exciting?" said Tara, Eddie's sister, as she hugged him from behind. "Finally! Your own dog! Can you believe it?"

It was incredible. Eddie had wanted a dog for as long as he could remember. "I can take care of it," Eddie had promised his parents when he was little.

Tara had rolled her eyes. Back then, she had just started high school. Mama was busy with her new publishing job. "Maybe next year" was what she always said about getting Eddie a dog.

After a lot of "next years," Eddie was finally here at the animal shelter. "Do you see one you like?" Mama asked. She seemed to want a dog as much as Eddie did, now that she worked at home, designing books in her own studio. She had begun to think that a dog might help keep her company while Eddie and Tara were off at school. Tara liked the idea of getting a dog, too. Even though she was away at college most of the year, she thought a dog might be fun to play with while she was home for the summer. Things should have been perfect.

Eddie walked up to a cage where a medium-size dog paced around excitedly. Eddie knelt down and peered in. The dog was white with patches of reddish brown on its sides. The dog came up and licked Eddie smack on the nose.

"This one?" asked Tara, kneeling next to Eddie. Mama and one of the shelter workers named Claire gathered around.

"That's a girl," Claire noted. "She's about eight months old. Her name is Ginger. We all love her—she's such a sweet dog."

Claire let Ginger out of the cage. The dog came right up to Eddie and put her paws on his shoulders. Across the way, he noticed a pair of poodle puppies scrambling to get out and join the fuss. In the next cage over, a basset hound howled. Eddie stood, patting Ginger on the head.

"What do you think?" Mama's face was as bright and wide as a full moon.

It seemed to Eddie that the more attention he paid to Ginger, the more upset the other dogs became. What would happen to them? They looked so lonely in this desolate place. He looked down at Ginger, sitting at his side as if she were already his. He looked up at Mama, Tara, and Claire.

Eddie shook his head. "I can't," he said miserably. He turned and walked out the door.

The next day, Eddie and Mama sat in Claire's office. "I called your mom yesterday after you left," Claire told Eddie. "I explained our fostering program to her. We could use someone like you."

"Fostering?" Eddie asked.

"It's our hope that we can match every dog here with a good home. A lot of dogs don't get adopted right away. While they wait, some of our dogs need more than we can give them at the shelter," Claire explained. "We place them with foster families."

"For how long?" Eddie asked.

"That depends," said Claire. "Sometimes it's just for a few days. With other dogs, it could be for a month or so."

"Then you—the foster family, I mean—don't
see the dog anymore?" Eddie asked.

"That's the hard part," said Claire, trying to
assuage his doubts. "You can't get too attached, but
the good part is that you can help a lot of dogs."

Claire explained that the shelter tried to find
foster families for very small puppies. Dogs that
seemed especially shy or afraid also needed special
care. Foster families also took in sick or hurt dogs.

The longer Claire talked, the more excited Eddie
became. He turned to Mama and asked, "Could we
be a foster family?"

Mama turned to Claire. "Can we start today?"

When they were ready to go, Eddie asked about Ginger. Claire told him that she had been adopted that very day. Sadness brushed lightly against him and then flitted away. Eddie had no time for sadness. Wrapped in a towel on his lap was a small black puppy. Someone had found him this morning and brought him to the shelter. Claire felt certain he would be adopted within a week. Still, he was barely old enough to leave his mother. It would be Eddie's job to take care of him until someone gave him a permanent home.

"Hey, little guy." Eddie petted the pup as he craned his neck to look around, curious about his surroundings. "Wait until you meet my big sister. Won't she be glad she's home for the summer!"

Tara did not return home until after supper. Then she bustled in and rushed straight to her room. "Don't come in, Eddie!" she called behind her closed door.

"Tara!" Eddie said. "You have to come see the little puppy we're taking care of." All afternoon, the puppy had slept peacefully in Eddie's lap. Sometimes he chewed on Eddie's shorts, gouging little holes in the hem with his teeth. When Eddie had to stand, the pup snored against his shoulder.

"I'll be out in a minute!" Tara shouted.

Eddie parked himself in the living room and stroked the puppy's sleek, black fur. There was no denying it. He was already in love with the little guy. Earlier, Claire had called to check on things. She had told Eddie's mother that a family was interested in adopting the puppy, though they wouldn't be ready to pick it up for another ten days. A surge of regret swirled in Eddie's heart. Was he really going to be able to handle loving a dog, only to give it up?

After a while, Eddie became aware of Mama and Tara whispering in the kitchen. "Eddie!" Mama called. "Come in here a minute!"

He got up slowly, cradling the puppy to his chest. In the kitchen, his mother and sister were standing behind the table with silly grins on their faces. This was odd—especially since the usually immaculate kitchen was now cluttered with dog stuff. A medium-sized dog crate sat on the floor, surrounded by dog bowls and some other things.

"Why did you bother to get all this, Tara?" asked Eddie. "The puppy is going to be gone in ten days! We don't need . . ."

Suddenly, Tara zoomed out from behind the table and snatched the puppy from Eddie. She was gentle about it, but the puppy woke up. "Is this him? Oooh—he's so cute!" Tara nuzzled the pup's nose. "It's going to be so hard to give you up, you little doll."

"Please don't remind me," Eddie sighed.

"You know what, Eddie?" asked Tara. "I think I have something that might make it easier. Especially if you're serious about doing this foster care thing."

Eddie felt his determination return. "I am," he said with renewed fervor.

Tara handed back the puppy. "Stay right here," she said as she walked out of the kitchen. When she returned a minute later, Eddie's jaw dropped. Walking beside her was an unexpected surprise.

"Ginger!" Eddie exclaimed. Eddie knelt down and threw his arms around his new dog. "I thought someone had adopted her already!"

"Someone did!" said Mama. "You! Well, Tara actually picked her up."

"Yup," said Tara. "I knew it was too hard for you to choose Ginger in front of all those other dogs, so I did it for you!"

As Eddie smiled gratefully at his sister, Ginger put her paw on Eddie and licked his face. Giving up a foster pup wouldn't be quite so difficult as long as he always had Ginger.

Think Critically

1. On his first trip to the animal shelter, why did Eddie walk out without choosing a dog?

2. How does the author describe Mama as she watches Eddie with Ginger at the shelter? Explain whether or not it is a good description.

3. What does Eddie's desire to foster homeless dogs tell you about his character?

4. Why does Tara end up adopting Ginger?

5. Do you think it is realistic for a boy like Eddie to help foster homeless dogs? Explain your opinion.

 ## Social Studies

Animal Foster Care Do research on the Internet or use other library sources to learn more about animal foster care. Summarize your findings in a paragraph.

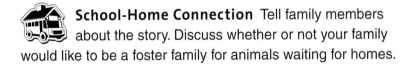 **School-Home Connection** Tell family members about the story. Discuss whether or not your family would like to be a foster family for animals waiting for homes.